5/9-

W9-BKE-030

THE SCARY BOOK

THE SCARY BOOK

Compiled by
Joanna Cole
and
Stephanie Calmenson

ILLUSTRATED BY

Chris Demarest   Marilyn Hirsh

Arnold Lobel   Dirk Zimmer

MORROW JUNIOR BOOKS

New York

To Amy Berkowitz

The authors wish to thank
Marian Reiner for her invaluable help
obtaining the permissions for this book.

Permissions for reprinting copyrighted material
are on page 125.

Library of Congress Cataloging-in-Publication Data
The Scary book / compiled by Joanna Cole and Stephanie Calmenson ;
illustrated by Chris Demarest...[et al.].
p.   cm.
Includes index.
Summary: A collection of spooky stories, poems, riddles, tricks,
and tongue twisters.
ISBN 0-688-10654-4
1. Supernatural—Literary collections.   [1. Supernatural—
Literary collections.]   I. Cole, Joanna.   II. Calmenson,
Stephanie.   III. Demarest, Chris L., ill.
PZ5.S325   1991
398.2—dc20   90-26330   CIP   AC

Contents

The Headless Man: Tricks, Games, and Other Spooky Things to Do

The Viper Is Coming

Stories

Strange Bumps

STORY AND PICTURES
BY ARNOLD LOBEL

Owl was in bed.

"It is time to blow out the candle and go to sleep," he said with a yawn.

Then Owl saw two bumps under the blanket at the bottom of his bed.

"What can those strange bumps be?" asked Owl.

Owl lifted up the blanket. He looked down into the bed. All he could see was darkness. Owl tried to sleep, but he could not.

"What if those two strange bumps grow bigger and bigger while I am asleep?" said Owl. "That would not be pleasant."

Owl moved his right foot up and down. The bump on the right moved up and down.

"One of those bumps is moving!" said Owl.

Owl moved his left foot up and down. The bump on the left moved up and down.

"The other bump is moving!" cried Owl.

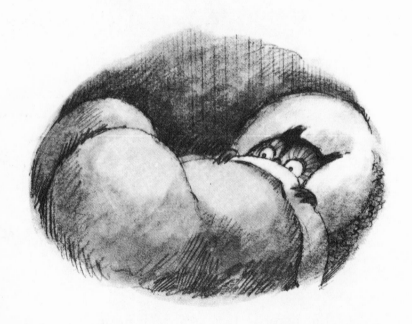

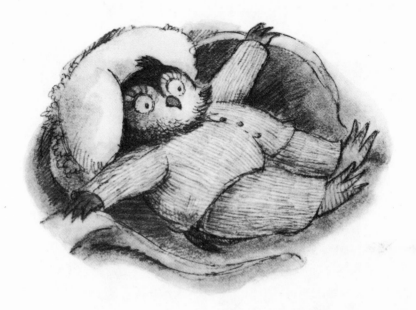

Owl pulled all of the covers off his bed. The bumps were gone. All Owl could see at the bottom of the bed were his own two feet.

"But now I am cold," said Owl. "I will cover myself with the blankets again."

As soon as he did, he saw the same two bumps.

"Those bumps are back!" shouted Owl. "Bumps, bumps, bumps! I will never sleep to-night!"

Owl jumped up and down on top of his bed.
"Where are you? What are you?" he cried.
With a crash and a bang the bed came falling
down.

Owl ran down
the stairs.
He sat in his
chair near the fire.
"I will let those two
strange bumps sit on my bed
all by themselves," said Owl.
"Let them grow as big as they wish.
I will sleep right here where I am safe."

And that is what he did.

Taily-po

RETOLD BY STEPHANIE CALMENSON

Once upon a time, in the big, deep woods, a man lived all by himself.

He had only one room and that room was his whole house: his sitting room, his bedroom, his dining room, and his kitchen too.

One night, while the man was sitting at his fireplace stirring his stew for supper, the most curious creature you ever did see fell—*bonk!*—right down the chimney. It landed on its head. And its great, big tail landed right in the man's stew pot.

"Yeowwee!" screamed that thing. Well, that scared the man so that he grabbed his axe and started swinging it. While he was swinging—*whoops!*—he chopped that thing's tail off. The thing turned around and clawed its way right back up the chimney.

"That was a close call," said the man. He went back to stirring the stew—tail and all. In a

18

little while, he sat down and ate. Then, with his stomach nice and full, the man went to bed and fell asleep in no time flat.

He hadn't been asleep very long when he was
awakened by the sound of something *stomping,
stomping, stomping* across the roof of his cabin.
Whoever was up there was really mad. By and by,
the man heard a voice say,

"*Taily-po, taily-po;*
Give me back my taily-po!"

Now the man would have been glad to give the tail back if he hadn't eaten it. But try explaining that to a creature stomping across the roof of your house.

So the man called his dogs, Uno, Ino, and Cumptico-Calico. "Here! Here! Here!" he said. The dogs jumped up from where they were sleeping and chased that thing back into the big, deep woods.

"Good dogs!" said the man. Then he pulled the covers up and went back to sleep.

In the middle of the night, the man was awakened again. This time, he heard something *creeping, creeping, creeping* down the side of his cabin. By and by, he heard a voice say,

"Taily-po, taily-po;
Give me back my taily-po!"

The man sat straight up and looked out the window. Sure enough there were two great green, upside-down eyes staring at him.

The man didn't wait one second before calling his dogs. "Here! Here! Here!" The dogs came bursting round the corner of the house. And they chased that thing away.

The man was shivering now from the sight of those great, green, upside-down eyes. This time he pulled the covers way up over his head before going back to sleep.

Just before daylight, the man was awakened
one last time. Something was *scratching, scratching,
scratching*—right at the foot of his bed!

The man peeked up over the covers. First he
saw two little pointed ears. Then he saw two great
green, right-side-up eyes. He tried to call his dogs.
"Here! Here! Here!" But he was so scared he had
no voice.

The next thing the man knew, that thing
pressed its nose right up to his and said,

"Taily-po, taily-po;
Give me back my taily-po!"

All at once the man got his voice back. "I
haven't got your taily-po!" he said. And that thing
said, "Yes you have."

Then the thing jumped on the man, turned
him upside down, and shook, shook, shook him.
And guess what? That tail fell right out, whole.

The man never saw that thing again. But if you visit him in the big, deep woods on a night when the moon shines bright and the wind blows cold, you'll hear a voice say,

"Taily-po, taily-po;
I got back my taily-po!"

Bony-Legs

BY JOANNA COLE

ILLUSTRATED BY DIRK ZIMMER

Bony-Legs was a horrible, bad witch. She could run very fast on her bony old legs. Her teeth were made of iron, and she liked to eat little children.

She lived deep in the woods in a hut that stood on chicken feet. All day long she waited for children to pass by.

On the edge of the same woods a girl named
Sasha lived with her aunt. One morning Sasha's
aunt sent her out to borrow a needle and thread.

Sasha took some bread and butter and a bit of
meat for lunch, and she began to walk. She walked
and walked. She was surprised when she came to a
hut that stood on chicken feet. But she decided to
go inside. She opened the gate. It creaked and
groaned.

"Poor gate," said Sasha. "You need some
grease." She scraped the butter from her bread and
rubbed it on the hinges of the gate. It opened
quietly.

Sasha walked up the path. A skinny dog stood
in her way. It barked and barked.

"Poor dog," said Sasha. "You look hungry."
She gave her bread to the dog. He ate it up and did
not bark again.

A cat was sitting near the hut mewing sadly.

"Poor kitty," said Sasha. "Are you hungry, too?" She gave her meat to the cat.

Old Bony-Legs poked her head out the window. "What do you want?" she asked Sasha.

"My aunt would like to borrow a needle and thread," said Sasha.

"Come right in," said the witch.

Sasha went inside.

"Now," said Bony-Legs, "get into the tub."

"Why?" asked Sasha. "I don't need a bath."

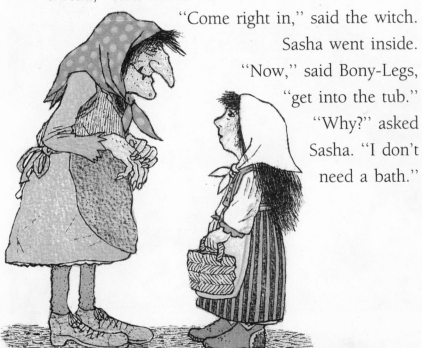

"I want you nice and clean," said Bony-Legs. "I'm going to cook you for my supper."

She grinned and showed her iron teeth. Then she went outside to gather sticks for the fire. She locked the door behind her. Sasha was scared. She began to cry.

"Don't cry," said a voice. "I will help you."

Sasha looked around. No one was there but the cat.

"Fill the tub but don't get in," said the cat.

Sasha had never heard a cat talk, but she did what it told her.

Bony-Legs called through the door, "Are you washing, girl?"

"Yes, I am," said Sasha.

"Good," said Bony-Legs. And she went away to gather more sticks.

After she had gone the cat gave Sasha a silver mirror.

"When you are in trouble, throw this away," said the cat.

That does not make sense, thought Sasha. But she took the mirror and put it in her pocket.

"Now run," said the cat.

Sasha climbed out the window and began to run.

The witch called through the door again, "Are you washing, girl?"

"Yes, I am," said the cat.

"Well, hurry up," said Bony-Legs. Then she went away.

Sasha ran through the yard. The dog stopped her and gave her a wooden comb.

"When you need help, throw this away," said the dog.

That does not make sense, thought Sasha. But she put the comb in her pocket. Then she opened the gate. It did not make a sound on its buttered hinges. Sasha ran into the woods.

Bony-Legs called through the door again, "Are you washing, girl?"

"Yes, I am," said the cat.

"What!" said Bony-Legs. "Not done yet?" She flung open the door.

There was the cat. There was the tub. But where was Sasha? "You sneaky cat!" yelled Bony-Legs. "Why did you trick me?"

"You never fed me," said the cat. "But Sasha gave me meat to eat."

"Bah!" said Bony-Legs, and she ran into the yard.

The dog was sleeping in the sun. "You lazy dog!" shouted Bony-Legs. "Why didn't you bark at her?"

"You never fed me," said the dog. "But Sasha gave me bread to eat."

"Bah!" said the witch, and she rushed to the gate. "You worthless gate!" she screamed. "Why didn't you lock her in?"

"You never took care of me," said the gate. "But Sasha put butter on my hinges."

The old witch flew into a rage. She stamped her feet, pulled her hair, and even pinched her own nose. But she did not feel any better.

She ran after Sasha on her bony old legs.
Sasha looked back and saw the witch's iron teeth
glinting in the sun. Sasha was scared. She remembered the silver mirror. She took it out of her
pocket and threw it behind her.

The mirror became a deep silver lake. Bony-Legs could not cross it.

She ran home and got her tub. She rowed it across the lake and ran after Sasha on her bony old legs.

Sasha saw the witch coming again. She remembered the wooden comb. She took it out of her pocket and threw it behind her.

The comb grew until it was as tall as three trees. Bony-Legs could not climb over it. She could not dig under it. She could not even squeeze through it.

At last she gave up. And she stamped her feet, pulled her hair, and pinched her nose all the way back to her hut.

Sasha went home, too. And you can be sure she never went back to the hut that stood on chicken feet.

And for as long as she lived she never saw old Bony-Legs again.

Wait Till Martin Comes

BY MARIA LEACH

That big house down the road was haunted. Nobody could live in it.

The door was never locked. But nobody ever went in. Nobody would even spend a night in it. Several people had tried but came running out pretty fast.

One night a man was going along that road on his way to the next village. He noticed that the sky was blackening. No moon. No stars. Big storm coming for sure.

He had a long way to go. He knew he couldn't get home before it poured.

So he decided to take shelter in that empty house by the road.

He had heard it was haunted. But shucks! Who believed in ghosts? No such thing.

So he went in. He built himself a nice fire on the big hearth, pulled up a chair, and sat down to read a book.

He could hear the rain beating on the win-

dows. Lightning flashed. The thunder cracked around the old building.

But he sat there reading.

Next time he looked up there was a little gray cat sitting on the hearth.

That was all right, he thought. Cozy.

He went on reading. The rain went on raining.

Pretty soon he heard the door creak and a big black cat came sauntering in.

The first cat looked up.

"What we goin' to do with him?"

"Wait till Martin comes," said the other.

The man went right on reading.

Pretty soon he heard the door creak and another great big black cat, as big as a dog, came in.

"What we goin' to do with him?" said the first cat.

"Wait till Martin comes."

The man was awful scared by this time, but he kept looking in the book, pretending to be reading.

Pretty soon he heard the door creak and a great big black cat, as big as a calf, came in.

He stared at the man. "Shall we do it now?" he said.

"Wait till Martin comes," said the others.

The man just leaped out of that chair, and out the window, and down the road.

"Tell Martin I couldn't wait!" he said.

The Rabbi and the Twenty-nine Witches

A TALMUDIC LEGEND
RETOLD AND ILLUSTRATED
BY MARILYN HIRSH

Once there was a little village where people were neither rich nor poor, good nor bad, wise nor foolish, except for the Rabbi, who was very wise. In this little village children went to school, cows gave milk, and grown-ups worked.

It was a very normal village except that under a nearby hill, in a deep, dark cave, there lived twenty-nine of the meanest, scariest, ugliest, wickedest witches that ever were.

There they lived and there they stayed, brewing their evil potions and raising their evil bats and buzzards. They practiced zooming around on broomsticks and screeching their hideous screeches.

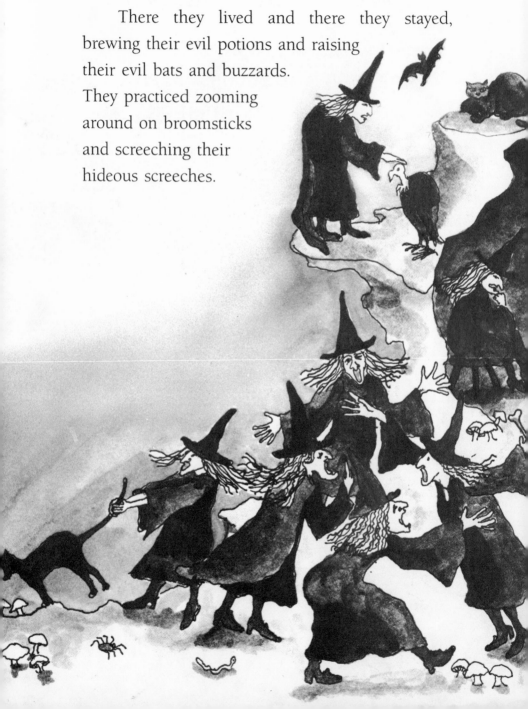

They pulled the tails of their cats and bit each other out of sheer nastiness. They turned flowers into poisonous mushrooms and planted them all around the cave.

But once a month, when the moon was full, the witches came out of their cave. They flew to the village and circled above it, shrieking and howling and laughing their horrible laughs. The cats yowled, the dogs yelped, the chickens laid cracked eggs, and the cows gave sour milk. The babies cried and everyone else had terrible witchy nightmares. But if it was raining on the night of the full moon, the twenty-nine witches did not come at all.

Now the next time the moon was full and it was not raining, everyone came home early. They locked their doors and bolted their shutters. Some hid under the bed. Others put pillows over their heads to drown out the creepy screeches.

People got born, grew up, and died without ever seeing the full moon.

Finally one old grandmother said, "I want to see the full moon before I die! Is that too much to ask?"

"Well," said her friend, "considering the witches it is quite a bit. We will go to the Rabbi and he will know what to do. After all, he is the Rabbi." So they did.

The Rabbi thought and thought about the problem. On the day before the next full moon, he reasoned, "If there is no full moon there are no witches, so there is no problem. But if there is a full moon there are witches and that is a problem. But if it rains on the night of the full moon there are no witches and there is no problem." He thought some more. "But if it rains on the night of the full moon there are no witches," he thought again. "That's it! I have a splendid idea," he cried out loud. "And I can try it out tomorrow night if the rain is still falling."

The Rabbi quickly called the grandmother to his side. "Have twenty-nine of the bravest men in the village come to me tomorrow night. Each one should bring a long white robe and a clay pot with a tight cover."

On the next night, as the rain was coming down, he said, "We are going to get rid of the twenty-nine witches once and for all. Put your robes carefully in the clay pots. Cover them tightly, for they must stay dry."

As brave as the men were, this was rather terrifying. But they trusted him for, after all, he was the Rabbi.

In the pouring rain they set out over the hills
to the dark, dangerous witches' cave. Each one carried his pot with his dry white robe in it. By the

time they got near the cave even the bravest one
was scared. Some say that the Rabbi looked a little
worried too.

They hid under a ledge near the cave. The Rabbi whispered, "I will go in first because, after all, I am the Rabbi. When I whistle once put on your robes. When I whistle again rush in and each of you pick up a witch. Start to dance with her. After that just listen to me." The Rabbi put on his long, dry, white robe and his most frightening expression and went into the cave.

"Witches, witches, I'm coming in," he cried.

"Whooo are youoooo?" they screeched.

"I'm one of youoooo," he cried.

He looked so scary that they said, "You do look like a witch but how did you stay so dry?"

"I walked between the raindrops," he said.

"What a trick," they cackled. "Doooo come in."

"Why have you come?" the chief witch scowled.

"Why not?" answered the Rabbi as bravely as he could. "You show me some magic and then I will show you some magic and we will all learn something."

"Why not?" said the witches.

So the Rabbi dared them to prepare him a wonderful feast.

One witch waved her wand and bread appeared. Another brought wine out of the air, and another brought fruit.

Soon there was a great table filled with plates and goblets, roasts and stews, cakes and cookies, soups and puddings, and every other good thing that there is to eat.

"So let's eat," said the Rabbi, forgetting for just a moment the reason he had come.

"Not so fast," said the chief witch. "Now show us some of your tricks."

"Ah yes," said the Rabbi slowly. "For my first trick I will produce twenty-nine handsome young men to dance with you at the banquet."

"That is quite a trick," cackled the witch. "No one has asked me to dance in four hundred years."

The Rabbi whistled
once and waited a minute. He
whistled again and in rushed
the brave men. Each grabbed
a witch and started to whirl
her around.

"And now for my greatest
trick of all," cried the Rabbi.
"I'll teach you to dance between
raindrops. Everyone outside."

The men picked up the witches
and carried them off into the rain.

"Youoooo tricked us," shrieked the witches in hissing, horrible, shrinking shrieks. For the Rabbi had figured out that witches must be afraid of the rain for a very good reason. As the men watched in amazement, the witches became smaller and smaller until they completely shrank away into nothing.

"It shouldn't happen to our worst enemies," said the men, for it was a sad sight to see.

But a good feast should not go to waste. So someone ran back to tell the people in the village that the witches were gone forever. Everyone came and danced and ate.

And on the night when the moon was full, all the people in the village from the oldest grandmother to the youngest baby came out to look. The cool, soft light turned the rooftops to silver. They all agreed that the full moon was very beautiful. When they had looked and looked for a long time everybody felt sleepy. So they went back to their houses and got into their beds and went to sleep. And nobody had any nightmares.

The Viper Is Coming

RETOLD BY STEPHANIE CALMENSON

The lady was home alone. She was not expecting any callers when the phone rang.

"Hello," said the lady.

"It's the viper," said a strange voice on the other end. "I'm coming to see you."

Click. The phone went dead.

The lady was shaken. She sat down to think. But not for long. Soon her downstairs buzzer was ringing.

"Who's there!" she shouted.

"It's the viper. I'm coming to see you," said the strange voice.

The lady fell into a chair. She sat in a frightened daze. The phone started ringing again.

"Hello," said the lady, hoping it was someone who could help. It wasn't.

"It's the viper," said the strange voice. "I'm on the first floor. I'll be there soon."

Whom could she call? No one. No one could

help her now. She sat. She waited. The phone started ringing once more. The lady answered.

"It's the viper. I'm on the second floor," said the voice.

The lady could hardly breathe. Before she knew it, the phone was ringing again.

"It's the viper," said the voice. "I'm on the third floor. I'm coming to see you now."

The lady's heart was pounding. It was all she could do to keep from screaming. Then there came a pounding at her door. She jumped back.

"Who is it! Who is it!" she cried.

"It's the viper!" said the voice. "I've come to vipe your vindows!"

hist

whist

Poems

BATTY

The baby bat
Screamed out in fright,
"Turn on the dark,
I'm afraid of the light."

Shel Silverstein

JOHNNY DREW
A MONSTER

John drew a monster.
The monster chased him.
Just in time
Johnny erased him.

Lilian Moore

THE FOSSILOT

You cannot find a Fossilot
Except in ancient stones,
Where imprints of its teeth and claws
Lie jumbled with its bones.

Some scientists cleaned up the bones,
Arranged, then tried to date them.
But when they had the jaw complete—
It turned around and ate them.

Jane Yolen

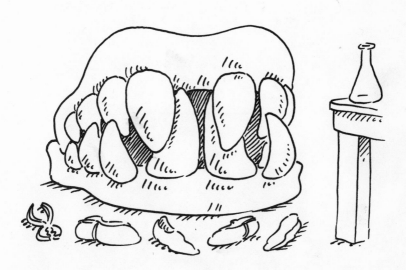

THE HALLOWEEN HOUSE

I'm told there's a Green Thing in there.
And the sign on the gate says BEWARE!
    But of course it's not true.
    That's why I'm sending you
To sneak in and find out—*but take care!*

John Ciardi

THE GOBLIN

A goblin lives in *our* house, in *our* house, in *our*
house,
A goblin lives in *our* house all the year round.
He bumps
And he jumps
And he thumps
And he stumps.
He knocks
And he rocks
And he rattles at the locks.
A goblin lives in *our* house, in *our* house, in *our*
house,
A goblin lives in *our* house all the year round.

Rose Fyleman

hist   whist

hist   whist
little ghostthings
tip-toe
twinkle-toe

little twitchy
witches and tingling
goblins
hob-a-nob   hob-a-nob

little hoppy happy
toad in tweeds
tweeds
little itchy mousies

with scuttling
eyes   rustle and run   and
hidehidehide
whisk

whisk　　look out for the old woman
with the wart on her nose
what she'll do to yer
nobody knows

for she knows the devil　　ooch
the devil　　　ouch
the devil
ach　　the great

green
dancing
devil
devil

devil
devil

　　　　wheeEEE

　　　　　　e. e. cummings

79

BOARDING HOUSE BLUES

At the boarding house where I live,
Everything is growing old.
Long, gray hairs are on the butter,
And the bread is green with mold.

When the dog died, we had sausage.
When the cat died, we had tea.
When the landlord died, I left there,
Spareribs were too much for me.

Old Folk Song

80

JACK'S GHOST

I had a little dog.
His name was Jack.
One day Jack died,
But his ghost came back.

He didn't want his collar.
He didn't want his ball.
He wanted his bones
And that was all.

Joanna Cole

HOW TO SPEAK SPOOK

Choose a night
when the wind's at work
shaking shutters,
rattling doors.
Invite black cats
to prowl the room.
Turn out the lights
and wait
until you feel
the moment's right.
Then yowl out
sounds so ghostly
even YOU know fright!
Practice boooo!
Stretch out that ooooh
like a balloon loooosing air.
And, if you dare,
scarenade your neighbors tooooooooooo.
To stop—
Chop off that oooooh.
One short sound of ooh will do.
Like—
BOO!

Joan Daniels Campbell

from THE OLD WIFE
AND THE GHOST

There was an old wife and she lived all alone
    In a cottage not far from Hitchin:
And one bright night, by the full moon light,
    Comes a ghost right into her kitchen.

About that kitchen neat and clean
    The ghost goes pottering round.
But the poor old wife is deaf as a boot
    And so hears never a sound . . .

From corner to corner he runs about,
    And into the cupboard he peeps;
He rattles the door and bumps on the floor,
    But still the old wife sleeps . . .

Madly the ghost tears up and down
    And screams like a storm at sea;
And at last the old wife stirs in her bed—
    And it's "Drat those mice," says she.

Then the first cock crows and morning shows
　　And the troublesome ghost's away.
But oh! what a pickle the poor wife sees
　　When she gets up next day.

"Them's tidy big mice," the old wife thinks,
　　And off she goes to Hitchin,
And a tidy big cat she fetches back
　　To keep the mice from her kitchen.

James Reeves

SLEEP-OVER

Marian
said
to pretend to sleep
and wait for her mother to go,
and then we could talk
the whole night long
and no one would ever know.

Marian
said
that the spooks come out
and climb through the window at night,
and she screamed four times
and woke everyone up
and she left on the bathroom
     light.

Marian
said
that the closet has ghosts
and she put a chalk hex on the door.
I slept over three times
at Marian's house,
but I'm not going there anymore.

Myra Cohn Livingston

THE WINTER GHOST

The ski suit, the muffler,
The heavy wool cap
Came up the Library stair.
And I tried to guess:
Is it boy? Is it girl?
I can usually tell by the hair.
But there was no face
And no other clue,
Though I stared as it passed,
With particular care.
So I peeked in the room
As it hung itself up—
There wasn't anyone there.

Pyke Johnson, Jr.

AUNT MAUD

I had written to Aunt Maud
Who was on a trip abroad,
When I heard she'd died of cramp
Just too late to save the stamp.

Author Unknown

IN MEMORY OF ANNA

Here lies the body of Anna
Done to death by a banana.
It wasn't the fruit that laid her low
But the skin of the thing that made
her go.

Author Unknown

IT ISN'T THE COUGH

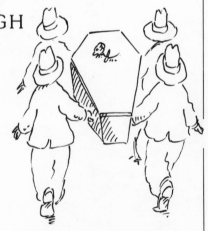

It isn't the cough
That carries you off;
It's the coffin
They carry you off in.

Author Unknown

The Headless Man

Tricks, Games, and Other Spooky Things to Do

The Headless Man Wants to Meet You

To play this trick on your friends, you will need:

- Large overcoat (stuff the shoulders with crumpled-up newspaper)
- Rubber knife (put some ketchup on it)
- Halloween mask of a person's head (stuff that with newspapers too)

Now ask your friends to sit in a room. Turn the lights down low and say, "Wait here for a minute. There's someone who wants to meet you."

Then go into the next room. Put on the overcoat, button the collar, and lift it up over your head. Hold the "bloody" knife in one hand and the mask in the other.

Start moaning in a deep voice, "Who cut off my head? Who cut off my head? I'm coming to get you!"

Then stomp into the room and watch your friends run!

(Note: Before you start, be sure to move any furniture out of the way, so you won't fall.)

Monster Teeth

Take an orange peel and ask an adult to help cut it as shown here. Then put it under your lips and over your front teeth so that the white side faces out.

Now find some friends, say hello, and watch them jump!

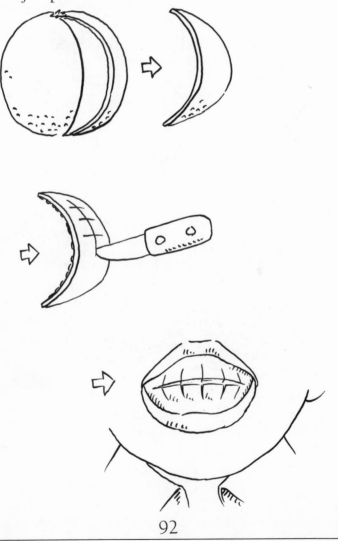

"I Found a Human Finger!"

This trick will really scare your friends!

First find a small box with a lid. Remove the lid and cut a hole in the bottom of the box big enough for your finger to fit through.

Put some cotton in the box and shake a little ketchup on it. Then put your finger through the hole. Slide on the lid. Now find a friend.

"You'll never guess what I found in the trash can behind school," you say. "A human finger!"

Then slide open the lid. There it is—a human finger, complete with blood!

The Hand of a Ghost

Here is how to trick a friend into thinking a ghost has touched her.

You have to be alone in a room with your friend. No one else can be there. Now sit across from your friend and say, "Just relax and do as I say, and a ghost will make contact with you."

Then stretch out your two index fingers toward your friend's eyes and say, "First, I am going to lay my fingers on your eyelids."

As your fingers get near, your friend will close her eyes. As soon as that happens, you pull a switch: You do not actually put the two index fingers on her eyes; instead, you put two fingers of *one* hand on her eyes. You say, "If you truly open your mind and open your heart, you will feel the presence of the spirit." And with your other hand, tap your friend gently on the shoulder.

Because your friend thinks both your hands are busy holding her eyelids, she will have the spooky feeling that a third hand—the hand of a ghost!—has touched her shoulder.

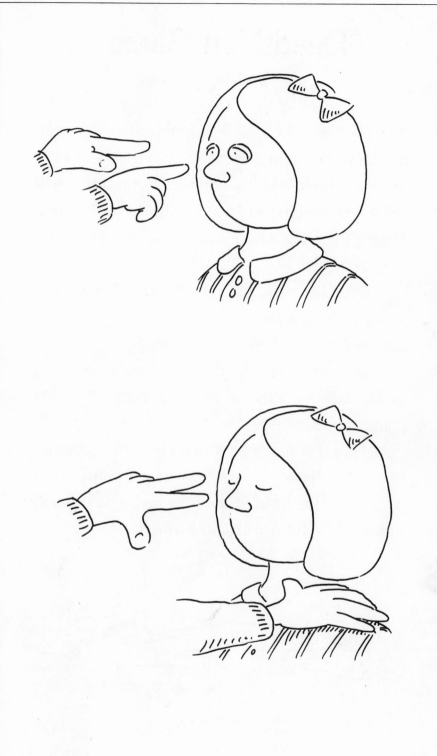

Dead Man Game

BY MARIA LEACH

Dead Man is a game played just for the scary fun of it. You and another friend or two already know the game and have prepared some objects to be passed from hand to hand in the dark. The more players there are who do *not* know the game, the more fun it is.

The players sit in a circle in the dark and speak in low, scary voices. No one can see. They can only hear and feel!

One says, "Here is the dead man's eye," and passes into the hand of the next player a peeled grape.

After that has gone round the circle, someone else says, "Here is the dead man's hand," and passes into the hand of the next player an ice-cold rubber glove filled with crushed ice.

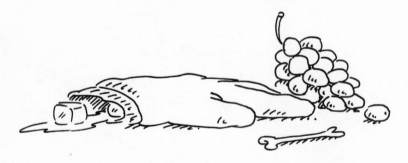

"Here are the dead man's brains," says another player, who passes a dish with a soft, squashy tomato in it.

Then another says, "These are the worms that crawled out of his skin," and passes a dish of wet, slippery, cooked spaghetti.

Somebody comes up with something new every time the game is played. A dried chicken bone, for instance, can be produced as the old skeleton's finger. An old piece of wet or greasy fake fur can be presented as the dead man's hair. And so on. What else can you think up?

How to Draw a Monster . . .

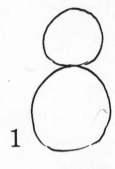

1

2 3

a Werewolf . . .

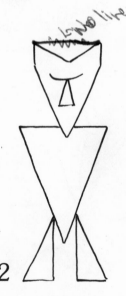

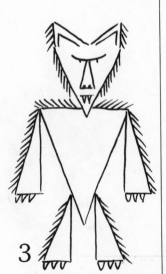

1 2 3

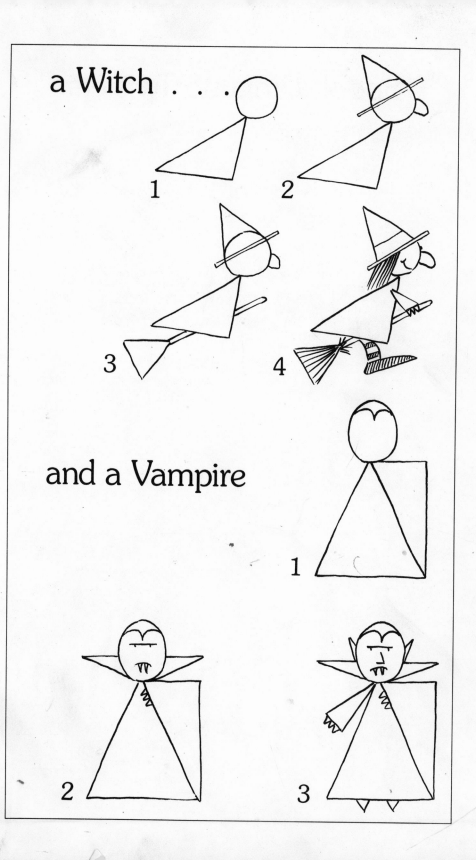

Spooky Tongue Twisters

Dracula dreads dead dwarfs.

Werewolves rarely roar.

Spooks scoop soup.

Green ghosts grin and glow.

Rich witches wear wristwatches.

Mummies make money.

The Ghost of John

This song is spookiest when sung in rounds. When the first singer comes to the end of the first line, the next singer begins.

THE GHOST OF JOHN

Arr. by Charnie Guettel

Have you seen the__ ghost of John?

Long white bones and the rest all gone.__

Ooh-oooooh,__ oo-oo- oo-ooh, ooh!

Would-n't it be chil-ly with no skin on?

Advice for Passing
a Graveyard

Avoid bad luck by doing one of the following:

- Hold your breath.

- Keep saying "bunny, bunny, bunny . . ." until you are past. Then say "rabbit."

- Hold your thumbs up. When you are past, turn your thumbs down.

Spook-a-doodle-doo

Jokes, Riddles, and Knock-knocks

Jokes and Riddles

SPOOK-A-DOODLE-DOO!

Q: What do ghost roosters say?
A: Spook-a-doodle-doo!

Q: Why did the ghosts get in the elevator?
A: They wanted to raise their spirits.

Q: What kinds of mistakes do ghosts make?
A: Boo-boos.

Q: Where do ghosts go swimming?
A: In the Dead Sea.

Q: What did the boy ghost say when he picked up his date?
A: My, you look boo-tiful!

Q: What is a ghost's favorite ride?
A: The roller ghoster.

MOMMY, MOMMY!

Little ghost: Mommy, Mommy! May I go out to play in the puddles?

Mother ghost: Of course, dear. As soon as you put on your ghoulashes.

Monster child: Mommy, mommy, I hate my teacher's guts!

Monster mother: Then leave them on the side of your plate.

Mother monster to baby monster: How many times must I tell you not to talk with your mouths full?

Mother vampire: What does a polite vampire always say?

Baby vampire: Please and fang you.

MUMMY, MUMMY!

Q: What does an Egyptian ghost call his parents?
A: Dead and Mummy.

Pharaoh: Are you *sure* your workers can build this pyramid right?
Architect: Of course. Our motto is "Satisfaction or your mummy back!"

Q: Why did the scientist quit her job studying mummies?
A: She was too wrapped up in her work.

IS THERE A MONSTER IN THE HOUSE?

Jane: What has six eyes, two noses, three ears, no mouth, and is sixty feet tall?

Bill: I don't know. But he just walked into your bedroom!

Waiter: We have a special this evening at ten dollars a head.

Diner: Perfect. I'll take two heads and a mixed salad of fingers and toes.

Q: How do you get King Kong to sit up and beg?

A: Wave a 500-pound banana in front of his nose.

Q: Why did the boy monster kiss the girl monster on the back of the neck?

A: That's where her lips were.

Rain poured down. Thunder crashed. Lightning flashed. A bridge collapsed, killing everyone on it.

"What a rotten night," said the monster. "It's good to be alive!"

Q: Do zombies like being dead?

A: Of corpse they do!

SPOOKS AT SC-GHOUL

Dracula: Why did you throw my son, Dracula Jr., out of school?

Principal: Because he was a pain in the neck.

Q: Why did Cyclops quit teaching?

A: He had only one pupil.

Q: Where did Madame Monster teach?

A: At an all-ghoul's school.

Q: What is a little witch's favorite subject in school?

A: Spelling.

NOW YOU ARE A B-A-T

CALLING DRACULA!

Q: What is the best way to call Dracula?
A: Long distance.

Q: How can you tell when Dracula has a cold?
A: He starts coffin.

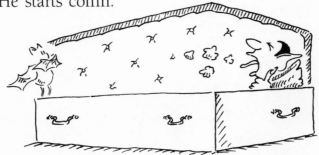

Q: Why did Dracula need a phone book?
A: He wanted to look up his neck-st victim.

Q: Did you hear about the new Dracula doll?
A: Wind it up and it bites Barbie on the neck.

YUM!

Q: What is a ghoul's favorite breakfast cereal?
A: Dreaded wheat.

Q: What is a witch's favorite lunch?
A: A sandwitch and a cup of alphabat soup.

Q: What is a ghost's favorite dinner?
A: Spookghetti.

Q: What is Dracula Jr.'s favorite candy?

A: An all-day sucker.

Q: What is a werewolf's favorite dessert?

A: Ladyfingers—real ones!

Q: What is a ghost's favorite candy?

A: Boo-ble gum.

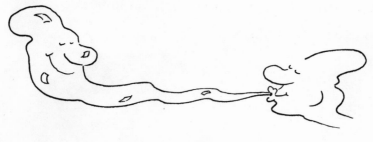

WHICH WITCH?

Q: What does a cool witch ride instead of a motor-cycle?

A: A brrrr-oomstick!

Q: Why did the witches cancel the baseball game?

A: They couldn't find their bats.

Q: How do you make a witch scratch?

A: Take away the *w*.

SILLY BONES

Q: How do you make a skeleton laugh?

A: Tickle its funnybone.

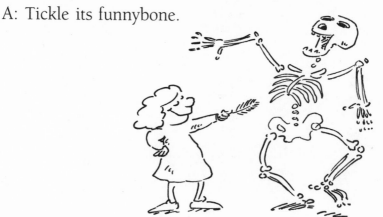

Q: Where does the largest population of American skeletons rest?

A: Tombstone, Arizona.

Q: How did skeletons send their letters in the old days?

A: By Bony Express.

GORY, GORY HALLELUJAH

Q: What do patriotic monsters sing?
A: *Gory, gory, hallelujah.*

Q: What's big, green, and mopey?
A: The Incredible Sulk.

Q: How did the vampire know he was in for a rotten day?
A: He looked at his horrorscope.

Q: Where do abominable snowmen like to dance?
A: At the snowball.

Q: What kinds of beans do cannibals like best?
A: Human bein's.

Q: What do you call a monster chasing a train full of people?
A: Hungry!

WHAT DO YOU GET?

Q: What do you get when you cross a ghost with a hen?

A: A see-through bird that says "Peck-a-boo."

Q: What do you get when you cross a skeleton with a jar of peanut butter?

A: Extra-crunchy peanut butter.

Q: What do you get when you cross King Kong with a frog?

A: A giant, hairy frog that hops up the side of the Empire State Building and catches airplanes with its tongue.

Monster Knock-knocks

BY WILLIAM COLE AND MIKE THALER

Knock knock.
  Who's there?
Howl.
  Howl who?
Howl I get in if you don't open the door?

Knock knock.
  Who's there?
Horror.
  Horror who?
Horror ya doin'?

Knock knock.

    Who's there?

Monster.

    Monster who?

C'monster the stew; it's stickin' to the pot.

Knock knock.

    Who's there?

Gruesome.

    Gruesome who?

Gruesome since I saw you last.

Knock knock.

Who's there?

Beast.

Beast who?

Beast still, I'm tryin' to think.

Knock knock.

Who's there?

Ghost.

Ghost who?

Ghost stand in the corner.

Acknowledgments

STEPHANIE CALMENSON. "Taily-po" and "The Viper Is Coming." Copyright © 1991 by Stephanie Calmenson. Used by permission of the author.   JOAN DANIELS CAMPBELL. "How to Speak Spook." Copyright © 1991 by Joan Daniels Campbell. Used by permission of the author.   JOHN CIARDI. "The Halloween House" from *The Hopeful Trout and Other Limericks* by John Ciardi. Text copyright © 1989 by Myra J. Ciardi. Reprinted by permission of Houghton Mifflin Company.   JOANNA COLE. "Bony-Legs" from *Bony-Legs* by Joanna Cole, illustrated by Dirk Zimmer. Text copyright © 1983 by Joanna Cole. Illustrations copyright © 1983 by Dirk Zimmer. Reprinted by permission of Four Winds Press, an imprint of Macmillan Publishing Company. "Jack's Ghost." Copyright © 1991 by Joanna Cole. Used by permission of the author.   WILLIAM COLE and MIKE THALER. "Monster Knock-knocks" from *Monster Knock-knocks* by William Cole and Mike Thaler. Copyright © 1982. Used by permission of the publisher, Pocket Books, a division of Simon & Schuster, N.Y.   E. E. CUMMINGS. "hist whist" is reprinted from *Tulips & Chimneys* by e. e. cummings, edited by George James Firmage. Copyright 1923, 1925 and renewed 1951, 1953 by e. e. cummings. Copyright ©1973, 1976 by the Trustees for the e. e. cummings Trust. Copyright © 1973, 1976 by George James Firmage. By permission of the Liveright Publishing Corporation.   ROSE FYLEMAN. "The Goblin" from *Picture Rhymes from Foreign Lands*. Copyright © 1935, 1963 by Rose Fyleman. Used by permission of the Society of Authors as the Literary representative of the Estate of Rose Fyleman. MARILYN HIRSH. "The Rabbi and the Twenty-nine Witches." Text and selected illustrations from *The Rabbi and the Twenty-nine Witches,* written and illustrated by Marilyn Hirsh. Copyright © 1976 by Marilyn Hirsh. All rights reserved. Reprinted by permission of Holiday House.   PYKE JOHNSON, JR. "The Winter Ghost." Copyright © 1991 by Pyke Johnson, Jr. Used by permission of the author.   MARIA LEACH. "Dead Man" from *Whistle in the Graveyard.* Copyright © 1974 by Maria Leach. Reprinted by permission of Viking Penguin, a division of Penguin Books USA Inc. "Wait Till Martin Comes" from *The Thing at the Foot of the Bed and Other Scary Tales* by Maria Leach. Copyright © 1959 by Maria Leach. Copyright renewed © 1987 by Macdonald H. Leach. Reprinted by permission of Philomel Books.   MYRA COHN LIVINGSTON. "Sleep-over" from *Worlds I Know and Other Poems* by Myra Cohn Livingston. Copyright © 1985 by Myra Cohn Livingston. Reprinted with permission of Margaret K. McElderry Books, an imprint of Macmillan Publishing Company.   ARNOLD LOBEL. "Strange Bumps." Text and specified art from "Strange Bumps" from *Owl at Home* by Arnold Lobel. Copyright © 1975 by Arnold Lobel. Reprinted by permission of Harper & Row, Publishers, Inc.   LILIAN MOORE. "Johnny Drew a Monster" from *Spooky Rhymes and Riddles* by Lilian Moore. Copyright © 1972 by Lilian Moore. Reprinted by permission of Scholastic, Inc.   JAMES REEVES. "The Old Wife and the Ghost" from *The Wandering Moon and Other Poems* (Puffin Books) by James Reeves. Copyright © by James Reeves. Reprinted by permission of the James Reeves Estate.   SHEL SILVERSTEIN. "Batty" from *A Light in the Attic* by Shel Silverstein. Copyright © 1981 by Evil Eye Music, Inc. Reprinted by permission of Harper & Row, Publishers, Inc.   JANE YOLEN. "The Fossilot" from *Best Witches* by Jane Yolen. Text copyright © 1989 by Jane Yolen. Reprinted by permission of G. P. Putnam's Sons.

Index

TITLE INDEX

AUTHOR AND ARTIST INDEX

JOANNA COLE

has taught elementary school and worked for a newsmagazine, and for several years was a senior editor for children's books. Today she is a full-time author, writing for and about children. She has written dozens of books, including *Bony-Legs, How You Were Born,* and the popular *Magic School Bus* series. She is also the compiler of several anthologies: *Best-Loved Folktales of the World, A New Treasury of Children's Poetry,* and *Anna Banana: 101 Jump-Rope Rhymes.* She lives in Connecticut with her husband and daughter.

STEPHANIE CALMENSON,

also a former teacher, and author of many books for children, has been the editorial director of *Parents* Magazine's Read Aloud Book Club. Her books include *The Children's Aesop, Fido, What Am I? Very First Riddles, Wanted: Warm, Furry Friend,* and *The Principal's New Clothes.*

TOGETHER,

Joanna Cole and Stephanie Calmenson have written *Safe from the Start: Your Child's Safety from Birth to Age Five,* and have compiled other anthologies for children, including *The Laugh Book, The Read-Aloud Treasury, Ready . . . Set . . . Read! The Beginning Reader's Treasury, Miss Mary Mack and Other Children's Street Rhymes,* and *The Eentsy, Weentsy Spider: Fingerplays and Action Rhymes.*

CHRIS DEMAREST

has written and illustrated several children's books, including *The Lunatic Adventures of Kitman and Willy* and *No Peas for Nellie,* which was nominated for the 1991 Colorado Children's Book Award. He also illustrated *The Butterfly Jar* by Jeff Moss.